LEARN JAVASCRIPT

100+ Coding Q&A

Yasin Cakal

Code of Code

CONTENTS

INTRODUCTION

Welcome to "Learn JavaScript," the ultimate book for anyone looking to master the world's most popular programming language. In this book you'll learn everything you need to know about JavaScript, from basic syntax to advanced techniques like asynchronous programming and working with APIs.

Whether you're a beginner looking to get started in web development or an experienced programmer looking to expand your skills, this book has something for you. With clear explanations, practical examples, and hands-on exercises, you'll be able to learn at your own pace and apply your new skills to real-world projects.

By the end of this book, you'll have a strong foundation in JavaScript and be able to build interactive, dynamic websites and web applications. So if you're ready to take your programming skills to the next level, join us in "Learn JavaScript" and start your journey to becoming a JavaScript expert today!

WHAT IS JAVASCRIPT AND WHY IS IT IMPORTANT?

JavaScript is a programming language that is used to make websites interactive and dynamic. It is the most popular programming language in the world, and it is supported by all modern web browsers.

A Brief History of JavaScript

JavaScript was first developed by Netscape in the mid-1990s as a way to add interactive elements to websites. It was initially released under the name LiveScript, but was later renamed to JavaScript to capitalize on the popularity of Java, another popular programming language at the time.

Since its inception, JavaScript has evolved and grown in popularity. It is now used to build all kinds of web applications, from simple websites to complex, data-driven web apps.

How JavaScript Works

JavaScript is a client-side programming language, which means that it is executed by the user's web browser rather than the web server. This allows JavaScript to run quickly and efficiently, as it does not have to rely on network requests to the server to perform its tasks.

JavaScript code is usually embedded in an HTML page and is executed when the page is loaded in the browser. It can also be used to manipulate the HTML and CSS of a page in real-time, allowing for dynamic and interactive elements such as drop-down menus, image sliders, and pop-up windows.

The Benefits of Learning JavaScript

There are many good reasons to learn JavaScript, regardless of your background or career goals. Here are a few:

JavaScript is Everywhere

As the most popular programming language in the world, JavaScript is used on an estimated 95% of all websites. This makes it an in-demand skill for web developers and a valuable asset for anyone looking to work in the tech industry.

JavaScript is Versatile

JavaScript can be used to build all kinds of web applications, from simple websites to complex, data-driven web apps. It can also be used to build mobile apps and desktop applications using tools like Cordova and Electron.

JavaScript is Constantly Evolving

The tech industry is constantly evolving, and JavaScript is no exception. New frameworks and libraries are being developed all the time, which means there is always something new to learn and explore. This keeps things interesting for JavaScript developers and helps them stay up-to-date with the latest trends and best practices.

Conclusion

JavaScript is a powerful and versatile programming language that is essential for anyone looking to work in the tech industry. Whether you are a beginner looking to get started in web development or an experienced programmer looking to expand your skills, learning JavaScript is a valuable investment in your career.

Exercises

To review these concepts, we will go through a series of exercises designed to test your understanding and apply what you have learned.

Explain the difference between client-side and server-side programming languages.
List at least three benefits of learning JavaScript.
Explain how JavaScript is used to make websites interactive and dynamic.
Research and list three popular JavaScript frameworks or libraries.
Search for a popular website and determine whether it uses JavaScript.

Solutions

Explain the difference between client-side and server-side programming languages.
Client-side programming languages are executed on the user's computer or device, while server-side programming languages are executed on the web server. This means that client-side languages do not need to rely on network requests to the server to perform their tasks, which makes them faster and more efficient. JavaScript is a client-side language, while languages like PHP and Ruby are server-side languages.

List at least three benefits of learning JavaScript.
- JavaScript is in high demand as a skill for web developers.
- It is versatile and can be used to build a wide range of web applications, as well as mobile and desktop apps.
- It is constantly evolving, which keeps things interesting for JavaScript developers and helps them stay up-to-date with the latest trends and best practices.

Explain how JavaScript is used to make websites interactive and dynamic.
JavaScript can be used to manipulate the HTML and CSS of a webpage in real-time, allowing for interactive elements such as drop-down menus, image sliders, and pop-up windows. It can also be used to respond to user events like clicks, hover, and form submissions, allowing for a more interactive and engaging user experience.

Research and list three popular JavaScript frameworks or libraries.
- React
- Angular

- Vue.js

Search for a popular website and determine whether it uses JavaScript.

For example, if we search for "Facebook" and inspect the page source, we can see that JavaScript is used heavily on the site. There are several references to JavaScript files in the HTML, and there is also inline JavaScript code that is used to manipulate the page and handle user events. This demonstrates the widespread use of JavaScript on modern websites.

SETTING UP A DEVELOPMENT ENVIRONMENT

Before you can start coding in JavaScript, you need to have a development environment set up on your computer. A development environment is a collection of tools and resources that you need to write, test, and debug your code.

In this article, we'll go over the steps you need to take to set up a development environment for JavaScript development.

Installing a Text Editor

The first thing you need is a text editor, which is a program that allows you to write and edit code. There are many text editors to choose from, each with their own features and capabilities. Some popular text editors for JavaScript development include:

- Sublime Text
- Visual Studio Code
- Atom

You can choose any text editor that you are comfortable with, as they all have similar features. Just make sure that it has syntax highlighting for JavaScript, which will make it easier to read and write code.

Installing a Web Browser

Next, you'll need a web browser to test your code. Any modern web browser will do, as they all support JavaScript. Some popular web browsers include:

- Google Chrome
- Mozilla Firefox
- Microsoft Edge
- Safari

You can use any of these browsers for JavaScript development, but it's a good idea to have more than one installed so you can test your code in different environments.

Installing Node.js

Node.js is a JavaScript runtime that allows you to run JavaScript on your computer outside of a web browser. It is a popular choice for developing server-side applications and command-line tools.

To install Node.js, visit the Node.js website and download the latest version. Follow the installation instructions for your operating system to complete the installation.

Setting Up a Local Development Server

A local development server is a program that runs on your computer and allows you to test your code in a simulated web server environment. This is useful for testing server-side code or for developing web applications that need to communicate with a server.

There are several local development servers available, but a popular choice is MAMP. MAMP is free to download and use, and it is available for both Mac and Windows.

To set up MAMP, download and install the program, then start the MAMP application. MAMP will automatically start a local web server and MySQL database server on your computer, which you can use to test your code.

Debugging Tools

Finally, you'll want to have some debugging tools at your disposal to help you troubleshoot any issues that may arise as you develop your code. Most modern web browsers have built-in developer tools that allow you to inspect and debug your code. To access the developer tools in Chrome, for example, you can right-click on any page element and select "Inspect" from the context menu.

Other popular debugging tools include:

- Firebug for Firefox
- Web Developer Extension for Chrome

Conclusion

Setting up a development environment is an important first step in JavaScript development. By installing the right tools and resources, you'll have everything you need to write, test, and debug your code. With a solid development environment in place, you'll be well on your way to becoming a JavaScript expert!

Exercises

To review these concepts, we will go through a series of exercises designed to test your understanding and apply what you have learned.

Explain the purpose of a text editor in a development environment.
List three popular web browsers that can be used for JavaScript development.
Describe the purpose of Node.js in a development environment.
Explain the purpose of a local development server in a development environment.
List two debugging tools that can be used in a development environment.

Solutions

Explain the purpose of a text editor in a development environment.
A text editor is a program that allows you to write and edit code. It is an essential tool for any developer, as it provides a workspace for writing and organizing code. Text editors typically have

features like syntax highlighting, code completion, and error checking to make it easier to write and understand code.

List three popular web browsers that can be used for JavaScript development.
- Google Chrome
- Mozilla Firefox
- Microsoft Edge

Describe the purpose of Node.js in a development environment.
Node.js is a JavaScript runtime that allows you to run JavaScript on your computer outside of a web browser. It is particularly useful for developing server-side applications and command-line tools.

Explain the purpose of a local development server in a development environment.
A local development server is a program that runs on your computer and simulates a web server environment. It allows you to test server-side code or develop web applications that need to communicate with a server. This is useful for testing and debugging code without the need to deploy it to a live server.

List two debugging tools that can be used in a development environment.
- Built-in developer tools in web browsers (e.g. Chrome DevTools)
- Firebug for Firefox
- Web Developer Extension for Chrome

VARIABLES AND DATA TYPES

In JavaScript, a variable is a named container that holds a value. Variables are used to store and manipulate data in your code.

In this article, we'll go over the basics of variables and data types in JavaScript, including how to declare variables, assign values, and work with different data types.

Declaring Variables

In JavaScript, you declare a variable using the var keyword followed by the variable name. Here's an example:

```
var message;
```

This declares a variable named message that currently has no value. You can also declare a variable and assign it a value at the same time using the assignment operator (=):

```
var message = "Hello, world!";
```

Data Types

In JavaScript, there are several data types that you can use to store different kinds of values. Here are the most common data types in JavaScript:

String

A string is a sequence of characters, such as words or phrases. Strings are declared using single or double quotes:

```
var message = "Hello, world!";
```
```
var name = 'John';
```

Number

A number is a numeric value. In JavaScript, there is only one type of number, which can be either an integer or a floating-point number. There is no separate data type for integers or decimals.

```
var age = 25;
```
```
var price = 19.99;
```

Boolean

A boolean is a value that is either true or false. Booleans are often used in control structures like ifstatements to test for certain conditions.

```
var isValid = true;
```

```
var isEmpty = false;
```

Null

The null data type represents a value that is intentionally empty or non-existent. It is different from an undefined value, which means that a variable has been declared but has not been assigned a value.

```
var user = null;
```

Undefined

The undefined data type represents a variable that has been declared but has not been assigned a value.

```
var user;
```

Type Coercion

In JavaScript, you can use variables to store values of different data types. For example, you can store a string in a variable and then later reassign it to a number:

```
var value = "10";
value = 10;
```

This is called type coercion, and it allows you to store different data types in the same variable. However, it can also lead to potential issues if you are not careful, as you may end up with unexpected results when performing operations on variables with different data types.

Conclusion

Variables and data types are essential concepts in JavaScript programming. By understanding how to declare variables, assign values, and work with different data types, you'll have a solid foundation for building interactive and dynamic web applications with JavaScript.

Exercises

To review these concepts, we will go through a series of exercises designed to test your understanding and apply what you have learned.

Declare a variable and assign it a string value.
Declare a variable and assign it an integer.
Declare a variable and assign it a boolean value.
Declare a variable and assign it a null value.
Assign a string value to a variable and then reassign it to a number value.

Solutions

Declare a variable and assign it a string value.

```
var message = "Hello, world!";
```

Declare a variable and assign it an integer.

```
var age = 25;
```

Declare a variable and assign it a boolean value.

```
var isValid = true;
```

Declare a variable and assign it a null value.

```
var user = null;
```

Assign a string value to a variable and then reassign it to a number value.

```
var value = "10";
```

```
value = 10;
```

OPERATORS AND EXPRESSIONS

In JavaScript, operators are special symbols that perform specific operations on values and variables. These operations can be arithmetic, logical, or assignment in nature.

Expressions are combinations of values, variables, and operators that evaluate to a single value. They are a fundamental part of any programming language and are used to perform calculations, make comparisons, and assign values.

In this article, we'll go over the different types of operators and expressions in JavaScript and how to use them in your code.

Arithmetic Operators

Arithmetic operators are used to perform basic arithmetic operations like addition, subtraction, multiplication, and division.

Here are the most common arithmetic operators in JavaScript:

- +: Addition
- -: Subtraction
- *: Multiplication
- /: Division
- %: Modulus (remainder)
- ++: Increment
- --: Decrement

Here's an example of how to use these operators in an expression:

```
var result = 3 + 5; // 8
result = result * 2; // 16
result = result / 4; // 4
result = result % 3; // 1
```

Comparison Operators

Comparison operators are used to compare values and return a boolean value of true or false.

Here are the most common comparison operators in JavaScript:

- ==: Equal to
- !=: Not equal to
- >: Greater than

- <: Less than
- >=: Greater than or equal to
- <=: Less than or equal to

Here's an example of how to use comparison operators in an expression:

```
var result = 3 > 5; // false
result = 3 >= 3; // true
result = "a" == "a"; // true
result = "a" != "b"; // true
```

Logical Operators

Logical operators are used to perform logical operations like and, or, and not.

Here are the most common logical operators in JavaScript:

- &&: And
- ||: Or
- !: Not

Here's an example of how to use logical operators in an expression:

```
var result = true && true; //
true result = true || false; // true
result = !true; //false
```

Assignment Operators

Assignment operators are used to assign values to variables. The most common assignment operator is the equal sign (=), which assigns a value to a variable.

There are also compound assignment operators that perform an operation and assign the result to a variable in a single step. These include:

- +=: Addition assignment
- -=: Subtraction assignment
- *=: Multiplication assignment
- /=: Division assignment

Here's an example of how to use assignment operators in an expression:

```
var result = 0;
result += 10; // 10
result -= 5; // 5
result *= 2; // 10
result /= 2; // 5
```

Operator Precedence

In JavaScript, some operators have higher precedence than others, which means they are evaluated before other operators. For example, the multiplication operator has a higher precedence than the addition operator, so the following expression:

```
var result = 2 + 3 * 4;
```

will evaluate to 14, not 20, because the multiplication is performed before the addition.

You can use parentheses to specify the order in which operations should be performed, like this:

```
var result = (2 + 3) * 4;
```

This will evaluate to 20, because the addition is performed first inside the parentheses.

Conclusion

Operators and expressions are an essential part of JavaScript programming. By understanding how to use different types of operators and how to create and evaluate expressions, you'll have the skills you need to build powerful and sophisticated web applications with JavaScript.

Exercises

To review these concepts, we will go through a series of exercises designed to test your understanding and apply what you have learned.

Use arithmetic operators to calculate the result of the following expression: (10 + 5) * 2 / 5.

Use comparison operators to compare the following values and assign the result to a variable: 5 and "5".

Use logical operators to evaluate the following expression: (true && false) || (true || false) && !false.

Use operator precedence to evaluate the following expression: 2 + 3 * 4 - 5 / 2.

Use parentheses to specify the order in which operations should be performed in the following expression: 2 + 3 * 4 - 5 / 2.

Solutions

Use arithmetic operators to calculate the result of the following expression: (10 + 5) * 2 / 5.

```
var result = (10 + 5) * 2 / 5;
// result = 15
```

Use comparison operators to compare the following values and assign the result to a variable: 5 and "5".

```
var result = 5 == "5";
// result = true
```

Use logical operators to evaluate the following expression: (true && false) || (true || false) && !false.

```
var result = (true && false) || (true || false) && !false;
// result = true
```

Use operator precedence to evaluate the following expression: 2 + 3 * 4 - 5 / 2.

```
var result = 2 + 3 * 4 - 5 / 2;
```

```
// result = 14
```

Use parentheses to specify the order in which operations should be performed in the following expression: 2 + 3 * 4 - 5 / 2.

```
var result = (2 + 3) * 4 - (5 / 2);
```

```
// result = 20
```

CONTROL STRUCTURES (IF/ ELSE, FOR AND WHILE LOOPS)

In JavaScript, control structures are blocks of code that allow you to control the flow of your program. They enable you to make decisions based on certain conditions and to repeat a block of code multiple times.

There are several control structures in JavaScript, including if/else statements, for loops, and whileloops. In this article, we'll go over the basics of each of these control structures and how to use them in your code.

If/Else Statements

An if/else statement allows you to execute a block of code if a certain condition is true, or another block of code if the condition is false.

Here's the syntax for an if/else statement:

```
if (condition) {
  // code to execute if condition is true
} else {
  // code to execute if condition is false
}
```

Here's an example of how to use an if/else statement:

```
var age = 25;
if (age > 18) {
  console.log("You are an adult.");
} else {
  console.log("You are a minor.");
}
```

In this example, the if block will be executed because the value of age is greater than 18.

You can also use multiple else if blocks to check for additional conditions:

```
var age = 25;
if (age < 18)
```

```
console.log("You are a minor.");
} else if (age < 21) {
 console.log("You are a young adult.");
} else {
 console.log("You are an adult.");
}
```

In this example, the else if block will be executed because the value of age is less than 21 but greater than or equal to 18.

For Loops

A for loop is used to execute a block of code multiple times. It consists of three parts: an initializer, a condition, and an incrementer.

Here's the syntax for a for loop:

```
for (initializer; condition; incrementer) {
 // code to execute
}
```

Here's an example of how to use a for loop:

```
for (var i = 0; i < 5; i++) {
 console.log("Hello, world!");
}
```

In this example, the for loop will execute the console.log statement five times, with the value of i starting at 0 and incrementing by 1 each time.

While Loops

A while loop is similar to a for loop, but it only has a condition. It will continue to execute a block of code as long as the condition is true.

Here's the syntax for a while loop:

```
while (condition) {
 // code to execute
}
```

Here's an example of how to use a while loop:

```
var i = 0;
while (i < 5) {
 console.log("Hello, world!");
```

```
i++;
}
```

In this example, the while loop will execute the console.log statement five times, with the value of istarting at 0 and incrementing by 1 each time.

Conclusion

Control structures are an essential part of JavaScript programming. By understanding how to use if/elsestatements, for loops, and while loops, you'll have the skills you need to build complex and interactive web applications with JavaScript.

Exercises

To review these concepts, we will go through a series of exercises designed to test your understanding and apply what you have learned.

Use an if/else **statement to check whether a number is even or odd.**
Use a for **loop to print the numbers 1 to 10 to the console.**
Use a while **loop to print the numbers 1 to 10 to the console.**
Use a for **loop to print the numbers 10 to 1 to the console.**
Use a while **loop to print the numbers 10 to 1 to the console.**

Solutions

Use an if/else **statement to check whether a number is even or odd.**

```
var num = 10;
if (num % 2 == 0) {
  console.log("The number is even.");
} else {
  console.log("The number is odd.");
}
```

Use a for **loop to print the numbers 1 to 10 to the console.**

```
for (var i = 1; i <= 10; i++) {
  console.log(i);
}
```

Use a while **loop to print the numbers 1 to 10 to the console.**

```
var i = 1;
while (i <= 10) {
  console.log(i);
  i++;
}
```

Use a for **loop to print the numbers 10 to 1 to the console.**

```javascript
for (var i = 10; i > 0; i--) {
  console.log(i);
}
```

Use a while **loop to print the numbers 10 to 1 to the console.**

```javascript
var i = 10;
while (i > 0) {
  console.log(i);
  i--;
}
```

DEFINING AND CALLING FUNCTIONS

In JavaScript, a function is a block of code that performs a specific task. Functions are an essential part of any programming language and are used to divide a larger program into smaller, more manageable pieces.

In this article, we'll go over the basics of defining and calling functions in JavaScript and how to use them in your code.

Defining Functions

To define a function in JavaScript, you use the function keyword followed by the function name and a set of parentheses. The function body is then placed inside curly braces.

Here's the syntax for defining a function:

```javascript
function functionName() {
  // code to execute
}
```

Here's an example of how to define a function that logs a message to the console:

```javascript
function sayHello() {
  console.log("Hello, world!");
}
```

You can also define a function with parameters, which are values that are passed to the function when it is called. The parameters are placed inside the parentheses, separated by commas.

Here's an example of how to define a function with parameters:

```javascript
function greet(name) {
  console.log("Hello, " + name + "!");
}
```

Calling Functions

To call a function in JavaScript, you simply use the function name followed by a set of parentheses. If the function has parameters, you pass the values to the function inside the parentheses, separated by commas.

Here's an example of how to call a function:

```
sayHello(); // logs "Hello, world!"
```
```
greet("John"); // logs "Hello, John!"
```

Return Values

A function can also return a value to the calling code. To do this, you use the return keyword followed by the value to be returned.

Here's an example of a function that returns a value:

```
function add(x, y) {
  return x + y;
}
```

You can then assign the return value of the function to a variable:

```
var result = add(2, 3); // result is 5
```

Conclusion

Functions are a powerful and useful tool in JavaScript programming. By understanding how to define and call functions, you'll have the skills you need to organize and reuse your code in a more efficient and effective way.

Exercises

To review these concepts, we will go through a series of exercises designed to test your understanding and apply what you have learned.

Define a function that takes two numbers as parameters and returns the sum of the numbers.
Call the function defined in exercise 1 with the arguments 3 and 4 and assign the result to a variable.
Define a function that takes a string as a parameter and returns the string with the first letter capitalized.
Define a function that takes an array as a parameter and returns the sum of all the elements in the array.
Call the function defined in the previous exercise with the argument [1, 2, 3, 4, 5]and assign the result to a variable.

Solutions

Define a function that takes two numbers as parameters and returns the sum of the numbers.

```
function add(x, y) {
  return x + y;
}
```

Call the function defined in exercise 1 with the arguments 3 and 4 and assign the result to a

variable.

```
var result = add(3, 4); // result is 7
```

Define a function that takes a string as a parameter and returns the string with the first letter capitalized.

```
function capitalize(str) {
  return str.charAt(0).toUpperCase() + str.slice(1);
}
```

Define a function that takes an array as a parameter and returns the sum of all the elements in the array.

```
function sum(arr) {
  var total = 0;
  for (var i = 0; i < arr.length; i++) {
    total += arr[i];
  }
  return total;
}
```

Call the function defined in the previous exercise with the argument [1, 2, 3, 4, 5]and assign the result to a variable.

```
var result = sum([1, 2, 3, 4, 5]); // result is 15
```

WORKING WITH OBJECTS AND OBJECT-ORIENTED PROGRAMMING

In JavaScript, an object is a collection of properties, each of which has a name and a value. Objects are used to represent real-world entities, such as people, places, and things.

Object-oriented programming (OOP) is a programming paradigm that is based on the idea of "objects", which can contain data and functionality. OOP is designed to make it easier to create and maintain complex software systems.

In this article, we'll go over the basics of working with objects and object-oriented programming in JavaScript.

Creating Objects

There are several ways to create an object in JavaScript. The most common way is to use the object literal syntax, which consists of a set of curly braces containing a comma-separated list of properties.

Here's an example of how to create an object using the object literal syntax:

```javascript
var person = {
  name: "John",
  age: 30,
  occupation: "developer"
};
```

You can also use the Object constructor to create an object:

```javascript
var person = new Object();
person.name = "John";
person.age = 30;
person.occupation = "developer";
```

Accessing Object Properties

To access an object's properties, you use the dot notation or the square bracket notation. The dot notation is generally easier to read and write, but the square bracket notation is more flexible and allows you to use variables to access the properties.

Here's an example of how to access object properties using the dot notation:

```
console.log(person.name); // logs "John"
```
```
console.log(person.age); // logs 30
```
```
console.log(person.occupation); // logs "developer"
```

Here's an example of how to access object properties using the square bracket notation:

```
console.log(person["name"]); // logs "John"
```
```
console.log(person["age"]); // logs 30
```
```
console.log(person["occupation"]); // logs "developer"
```

You can also use variables with the square bracket notation:

```
var property = "name";
```
```
console.log(person[property]); // logs "John"
```

Modifying Object Properties

To modify an object's properties, you simply assign a new value to the property.

Here's an example of how to modify an object property:

```
person.age = 31;
```
```
console.log(person.age); // logs 31
```

Adding and Removing Object Properties

To add a new property to an object, you simply assign a value to a property that doesn't already exist.

Here's an example of how to add a new property to an object:

```
person.email = "john@example.com";
```
```
console.log(person.email); // logs "john@example.com"
```

To remove a property from an object, you can use the delete operator.

Here's an example of how to remove a property from an object:

```
delete person.email;
```
```
console.log(person.email); // logs undefined
```

Object-Oriented Programming

Object-oriented programming (OOP) is a programming paradigm that is based on the idea of "objects", which can contain data and functionality. OOP is designed to make it easier to create and maintain complex software systems.

In JavaScript, you can use OOP by defining "classes" which serve as templates for creating "instances" of objects. A class is defined using the class keyword followed by the class name and a set of curly braces containing the class properties and methods.

Here's an example of how to define a class in JavaScript:

```
class Person {
 constructor(name, age, occupation) {
  this.name = name;
  this.age = age;
  this.occupation = occupation;
 }
 greet() {
  console.log("Hello, my name is " + this.name + " and I am a " + this.occupation + ".");
 }
}
```

To create an instance of an object, you use the new operator followed by the class name and a set of parentheses containing the constructor arguments.

Here's an example of how to create an instance of an object:

```
var john = new Person("John", 30, "developer");
```

You can then access the object's properties and methods using the dot notation:

```
console.log(john.name); // logs "John"
console.log(john.age); // logs 30
console.log(john.occupation); // logs "
john.greet();
// logs "Hello, my name is John and I am a developer."
```

Inheritance

In OOP, you can use inheritance to create a "child" class that derives properties and methods from a "parent" class. This allows you to reuse code and avoid repeating yourself.

In JavaScript, you can use inheritance by using the extends keyword to create a child class that extends a parent class. The child class can then override or add additional properties and methods as needed.

Here's an example of how to use inheritance in JavaScript:

```
class Employee extends Person {
 constructor(name, age, occupation, company) {
  super(name, age, occupation);
  this.company = company;
 }
```

```
work() {
    console.log("I am working at " + this.company + ".");
}
}
var jane = new Employee("Jane", 32, "developer", "Acme Inc.");
console.log(jane.name); // logs "Jane"
console.log(jane.age); // logs 32
console.log(jane.occupation); // logs "developer"
console.log(jane.company); // logs "Acme Inc."
jane.greet(); // logs "Hello, my name is Jane and I am a developer."
jane.work(); // logs "I am working at Acme Inc."
```

In this example, the Employee class extends the Person class and adds a new company property and a new work method. The Employee class also overrides the constructor method to include the company argument and calls the super function to access the parent class's constructor method.

Conclusion

Objects and object-oriented programming are powerful tools in JavaScript. By understanding how to create and manipulate objects, as well as how to use inheritance, you'll have the skills you need to create complex and scalable software systems in JavaScript.

Exercises

To review these concepts, we will go through a series of exercises designed to test your understanding and apply what you have learned.

Define an object that represents a book, including the title, author, and number of pages.
Modify the object defined in exercise 1 to include a read property that is a boolean indicating whether or not the book has been read.
Define a class that represents a person, including the person's name, age, and occupation. Add a method to the class that logs a greeting to the console.
Create an instance of the class defined in exercise 3 and call the greet method.
Define a class that represents an employee, which extends the person class defined in exercise 3. Add a method to the employee class that logs the employee's company.

Solutions

Define an object that represents a book, including the title, author, and number of pages.

```
var book = {
    title: "The Great Gatsby",
    author: "F. Scott Fitzgerald",
    pages: 180
};
```

Modify the object defined in exercise 1 to include a read property that is a boolean indicating whether or not the book has been read.

```
book.read = false;
```

Define a class that represents a person, including the person's name, age, and occupation. Add a method to the class that logs a greeting to the console.

```
class Person {
  constructor(name, age, occupation) {
    this.name = name;
    this.age = age;
    this.occupation = occupation;
  }
  greet() {
    console.log("Hello, my name is " + this.name + " and I am a " + this.occupation + ".");
  }
}
```

Create an instance of the class defined in exercise 3 and call the greet method.

```
var john = new Person("John", 30, "developer");
john.greet(); // logs "Hello, my name is John and I am a developer."
```

Define a class that represents an employee, which extends the person class defined in exercise 3. Add a method to the employee class that logs the employee's company.

```
class Employee extends Person {
  constructor(name, age, occupation, company) {
    super(name, age, occupation);
    this.company = company;
  }
  work() {
    console.log("I am working at " + this.company + ".");
  }
}
```

UNDERSTANDING THE DOCUMENT OBJECT MODEL (DOM)

The Document Object Model (DOM) is a programming interface for HTML and XML documents. It represents the structure of a document as a tree of objects, with each object representing an element in the document.

The DOM allows you to manipulate the content and structure of a document using JavaScript. This enables you to create dynamic and interactive web pages that can respond to user input and changing data.

In this article, we'll go over the basics of the DOM and how to use it in JavaScript.

The DOM Tree

The DOM represents a document as a tree of objects, with the document itself at the root of the tree. Each object in the tree represents an element in the document, such as a paragraph, a link, or a form.

The tree structure of the DOM is called the "DOM tree". The DOM tree consists of "nodes", with each node representing an object in the tree. There are several types of nodes in the DOM, including element nodes, attribute nodes, and text nodes.

Here's an example of a simple HTML document and its corresponding DOM tree:

```
<html>
  <head>
    <title>My Page</title>
  </head>
  <body>
    <h1>Welcome to My Page</h1>
    <p>This is a paragraph.</p>
  </body>
</html>
     root node
       |
       html node
```

```
    /     \
head node   body node
    /    \
  h1 node    p node
```

Accessing DOM Elements

To access DOM elements in JavaScript, you can use the document object and various methods and properties.

The document.getElementById method allows you to access an element by its unique id attribute. Here's an example of how to use document.getElementById:

```
var header = document.getElementById("header");
```

The document.getElementsByTagName method allows you to access a collection of elements by their tag name. Here's an example of how to use document.getElementsByTagName:

```
var paragraphs = document.getElementsByTagName("p");
```

The document.getElementsByClassName method allows you to access a collection of elements by their class name. Here's an example of how to use document.getElementsByClassName:

```
var highlighted = document.getElementsByClassName("highlighted");
```

You can also use the document.querySelector and document.querySelectorAll methods to access elements using CSS selectors. Here's an example of how to use document.querySelector:

```
var header = document.querySelector("#header");
```

And here's an example of how to use document.querySelectorAll:

```
var highlighted =
document.querySelectorAll(".highlighted");
```

Modifying DOM Elements

Once you have access to a DOM element, you can modify its content and attributes using various methods and properties.

To modify the content of an element, you can use the innerHTML property. Here's an example of how to use innerHTML:

```
header.innerHTML = "Welcome to My New Page";
```

To modify the attributes of an element, you can use the setAttribute method. Here's an example of how to use setAttribute:

```
header.setAttribute("class", "new-class");
```

You can also use the style property to modify the CSS styles of an element. Here's an example of how to use the style property:

```
header.style.color = "red";
```

Adding and Removing DOM Elements

The DOM allows you to add and remove elements from the document using various methods.

To add an element to the document, you can use the createElement method to create a new element and the appendChild method to append the element to an existing element. Here's an example of how to add an element to the document:

```
var newParagraph = document.createElement("p");
newParagraph.innerHTML = "This is a new paragraph.";
document.body.appendChild(newParagraph);
```

To remove an element from the document, you can use the removeChild method. Here's an example of how to remove an element from the document:

```
document.body.removeChild(newParagraph);
```

Conclusion

The DOM is an essential part of JavaScript and enables you to create dynamic and interactive web pages. By understanding how to access and modify DOM elements, you'll have the skills you need to create powerful and engaging web applications.

Exercises

To review these concepts, we will go through a series of exercises designed to test your understanding and apply what you have learned.

Use the document.getElementById method to access the element with the id "header" and change its innerHTML to "Welcome to My New Page".

Use the document.getElementsByTagName method to access all the p elements in the document and change their innerHTML to "This is a new paragraph."

Use the document.createElement and appendChild methods to add a new p element to the end of the body element.

Use the document.querySelector method to access the element with the class"highlighted" and change its style.color to "red".

Use the removeChild method to remove the element created in exercise 3 from the bodyelement.

Solutions

Use the document.getElementById method to access the element with the id "header" and change its innerHTML to "Welcome to My New Page".

```
var header = document.getElementById("header");
header.innerHTML = "Welcome to My New Page";
```

Use the document.getElementsByTagName method to access all the p elements in the document and change their innerHTML to "This is a new paragraph."

```
var paragraphs = document.getElementsByTagName("p");
for (var i = 0; i < paragraphs.length; i++) {
 paragraphs[i].innerHTML = "This is a new paragraph.";
}
```

Use the document.createElement and appendChild methods to add a new p element to the end of the body element.

```
var newParagraph = document.createElement("p");
newParagraph.innerHTML = "This is a new paragraph.";
document.body.appendChild(newParagraph);
```

Use the document.querySelector method to access the element with the class"highlighted" and change its style.color to "red".

```
var highlighted = document.querySelector(".highlighted");
highlighted.style.color = "red";
```

Use the removeChild method to remove the element created in exercise 3 from the bodyelement.

```
document.body.removeChild(newParagraph);
```

MANIPULATING HTML ELEMENTS WITH JAVASCRIPT

JavaScript allows you to manipulate HTML elements and change the content, attributes, and styles of a web page. This enables you to create dynamic and interactive web pages that can respond to user input and changing data.

In this article, we'll go over the different ways you can manipulate HTML elements with JavaScript, including using the Document Object Model (DOM), working with HTML forms, and creating and modifying CSS styles.

The Document Object Model (DOM)

The Document Object Model (DOM) is a programming interface for HTML and XML documents. It represents the structure of a document as a tree of objects, with each object representing an element in the document.

You can use the DOM to access and modify HTML elements in JavaScript. This is done by using the document object and various methods and properties, such as getElementById, getElementsByTagName, and querySelector.

Here's an example of how to use the DOM to change the content of an element:

```
var header = document.getElementById("header");
header.innerHTML = "Welcome to My New Page";
```

And here's an example of how to use the DOM to change the attributes of an element:

```
header.setAttribute("class", "new-class");
```

Working with HTML Forms

HTML forms allow you to gather user input and send it to a server. You can use JavaScript to access and manipulate form elements, such as text fields, radio buttons, and select lists.

To access a form element in JavaScript, you can use the document.getElementById method. Here's an example of how to access a text field in a form:

```
var textField = document.getElementById("text-field");
```

You can then use various methods and properties to manipulate the form element. For example, you can use the value property to get or set the value of a text field:

```
textField.value = "Hello World!";
```

You can also use the checked property to get or set the checked state of a radio button or checkbox:

```
var radioButton =
document.getElementById("radio-button");
radioButton.checked = true;
```

Creating and Modifying CSS Styles

You can use JavaScript to create and modify CSS styles for HTML elements. This allows you to change the appearance of a web page in response to user input or changing data.

To change the CSS styles of an element, you can use the styleproperty and set the desired CSS properties. Here's an example of how to change the color of an element:

```
var header = document.getElementById("header");
header.style.color = "red";
```

You can also use the className property to add or remove CSS classes from an element. Here's an example of how to add a CSS class to an element:

```
header.className += " highlighted";
```

And here's an example of how to remove a CSS class from an element:

```
header.className = header.className.replace(" highlighted", "");
```

Conclusion

Manipulating HTML elements with JavaScript allows you to create dynamic and interactive web pages. By understanding how to use the DOM, work with HTML forms, and create and modify CSS styles, you'll have the skills you need to create powerful and engaging web applications.

Exercises

To review these concepts, we will go through a series of exercises designed to test your understanding and apply what you have learned.

Use the DOM to access the element with the id"header" and change its innerHTML to "Welcome to My New Page".
Use the DOM to access the text field in a form and set its value to "Hello World!".
Use the DOM to access a radio button in a form and set its checked property to true.
Use the style property to change the color of an element with the id "header" to "red".
Use the className property to add the CSS class "highlighted" to an element with the id "header".

Solutions

Use the DOM to access the element with the id"header" and change its innerHTML to "Welcome to My New Page".

```
var header = document.getElementById("header");
header.innerHTML = "Welcome to My New Page";
```

Use the DOM to access the text field in a form and set its value **to "Hello World!".**

```
var textField = document.getElementById("text-field");
textField.value = "Hello World!";
```

Use the DOM to access a radio button in a form and set its checked **property to** true.

```
var radioButton = document.getElementById("radio-button");
radioButton.checked = true;
```

Use the style **property to change the** color **of an element with the** id **"header" to "red".**

```
var header = document.getElementById("header");
header.style.color = "red";
```

Use the className **property to add the CSS class "highlighted" to an element with the** id **"header".**

```
header.className += " highlighted";
```

RESPONDING TO USER EVENTS (CLICK, HOVER, ETC.)

User events are actions that users take on a web page, such as clicking a button, hovering over an element, or typing in a text field. You can use JavaScript to respond to these events and create dynamic and interactive web pages.

In this article, we'll go over the different types of user events in JavaScript and how to use them to create interactive web pages.

Click Events

Click events are triggered when a user clicks on an element. You can use the click event to respond to a user's click and perform an action, such as displaying a message or changing the content of an element.

To attach a click event to an element, you can use the addEventListener method. Here's an example of how to attach a click event to a button:

```
var button = document.getElementById("button");
button.addEventListener("click", function() {
 alert("Button clicked!");
});
```

You can also use the onclick attribute to attach a click event to an element. Here's an example of how to use the onclick attribute:

```
<button id="button"
onclick="alert('Button clicked!')">Click Me</button>
```

Hover Events

Hover events are triggered when a user moves their mouse over an element. You can use the mouseoverand mouseout events to respond to a user's hover and perform an action, such as changing the appearance of an element.

To attach a hover event to an element, you can use the addEventListener method. Here's an example of how to attach a hover event to a div element:

```
var div = document.getElementById("div");
```

```
div.addEventListener("mouseover", function() {
  div.style.backgroundColor = "yellow";
});
div.addEventListener("mouseout", function() {
  div.style.backgroundColor = "white";
});
```

You can also use the onmouseover and onmouseout attributes to attach hover events to an element. Here's an example of how to use the onmouseover and onmouseout attributes:

```
<div id="div"
onmouseover="this.style.backgroundColor = 'yellow'"
onmouseout="this.style.backgroundColor = 'white'">
Hover over me</div>
```

Key Events

Key events are triggered when a user types on their keyboard. You can use the keydown, keyup, and keypress events to respond to a user's keyboard input and perform an action, such as validating a form field or searching for content.

To attach a key event to an element, you can use the addEventListener method. Here's an example of how to attach a key event to a text field:

```
var textField = document.getElementById("text-field");
textField.addEventListener("keydown", function() {
  console.log("Key down!");
});
textField.addEventListener("keyup", function() {
  console.log("Key up!");
});
textField.addEventListener("keypress", function() {
  console.log("Key press!");
});
```

You can also use the onkeydown, onkeyup, and onkeypress attributes to attach key events to an element. Here's an example of how to use the onkeydown, onkeyup, and onkeypress attributes:

```
<input id="text-field" type="text"
onkeydown="console.log('Key down!')"
onkeyup="console.log('Key up!')"
onkeypress="console.log('Key press!')">
```

Conclusion

User events are a crucial part of creating interactive and dynamic web pages. By understanding how to use different events, such as click, hover, and key events, you'll have the skills you need to create engaging and responsive web applications.

Exercises

To review these concepts, we will go through a series of exercises designed to test your understanding and apply what you have learned.

Use the `addEventListener` method to attach a click event to a button that displays an alert message when clicked.
Use the `onmouseover` and `onmouseout` attributes to attach hover events to a div element that changes the background color when hovered over.
Use the `addEventListener` method to attach key events to a text field that logs a message to the console when a key is pressed.
Use the `addEventListener` method to attach a click event to a button that changes the text of a div element when clicked.
Use the `onmouseover` and `onmouseout` attributes to attach hover events to a div element that toggles a CSS class when hovered over.

Solutions

Use the `addEventListener` method to attach a click event to a button that displays an alert message when clicked.

```javascript
var button = document.getElementById("button");
button.addEventListener("click", function() {
  alert("Button clicked!");
});
```

Use the `onmouseover` and `onmouseout` attributes to attach hover events to a div element that changes the background color when hovered over.

```html
<div id="div"
onmouseover="this.style.backgroundColor =
'yellow'"
onmouseout="this.style.backgroundColor =
'white'">Hover over me</div>
```

Use the `addEventListener` method to attach key events to a text field that logs a message to the console when a key is pressed.

```javascript
var textField = document.getElementById("text-field");
textField.addEventListener("keydown", function() {
  console.log("Key down!");
});
```

```
textField.addEventListener("keyup", function() {
  console.log("Key up!");
});
textField.addEventListener("keypress", function() {
  console.log("Key press!");
});
```

Use the addEventListener **method to attach a click event to a button that changes the text of a div element when clicked.**

```
var button = document.getElementById("button");
var div = document.getElementById("div");
button.addEventListener("click", function() {
  div.innerHTML = "Button clicked!";
});
```

Use the onmouseover **and** onmouseout **attributes to attach hover events to a div element that toggles a CSS class when hovered over.**

```
<style>
.highlighted {
  background-color: yellow;
}
</style>
<div              id="div"                onmouseover="this.classList.add('highlighted')"
onmouseout="this.classList.remove('highlighted')">Hover over me</div>
```

WORKING WITH ARRAYS AND COLLECTIONS

Arrays and collections are data structures that allow you to store and manipulate a group of values. They are an essential part of JavaScript programming and can be used to store a wide variety of data types, including numbers, strings, objects, and more.

In this article, we'll go over the basics of arrays and collections in JavaScript and how to use them to store and manipulate data.

Arrays

An array is an ordered collection of values. You can create an array in JavaScript by enclosing a comma-separated list of values in square brackets []. Here's an example of how to create an array of numbers:

```
var numbers = [1, 2, 3, 4, 5];
```

You can access the values in an array by using the array's index. Array indices start at 0, so to access the first element of an array, you would use the index 0. Here's an example of how to access the first element of an array:

```
var firstElement = numbers[0];
// firstElement is 1
```

You can also use the length property to get the number of elements in an array:

```
var numberOfElements = numbers.length;
// numberOfElements is 5
```

Modifying Arrays

You can use various methods to modify the values in an array. Here are a few examples:

- The push method adds an element to the end of an array:

```
numbers.push(6);
// numbers is now [1, 2, 3, 4, 5, 6]
```

- The unshift method adds an element to the beginning of an array:

```
numbers.unshift(0);
// numbers is now [0, 1, 2, 3, 4, 5, 6]
```

- The splice method removes elements from an array and, optionally, adds new elements:

```
numbers.splice(3, 2);
// numbers is now [0, 1, 2, 5, 6]
numbers.splice(3, 0, 3, 4);
// numbers is now [0, 1, 2, 3, 4, 5, 6]
```

Iterating Over Arrays

You can use a for loop to iterate over the elements of an array. Here's an example of how to use a for loop to iterate over an array:

```
for (var i = 0; i < numbers.length; i++) {
  console.log(numbers[i]);
}
```

You can also use the forEach method to iterate over an array. The forEach method takes a callback function as an argument, and the callback function is called for each element in the array. Here's an example of how to use the forEach method:

```
numbers.forEach(function(number) {
  console.log(number);
});
```

Collections

In addition to arrays, JavaScript also has several built-in collection types, including Set, Map, and WeakMap.

A Set is a collection of unique values, meaning that it cannot contain duplicate values. You can create a Setby using the Set constructor.

Here's an example of how to create a Set and add items to it:

```
var set = new Set();
set.add(1);
set.add(2);
set.add(3);
```

You can use the size property to get the number of items in a Set, and the has method to check if a Setcontains a specific value.

Here's an example of how to use the size property and the has method:

```
console.log(set.size); // 3
console.log(set.has(1)); // true
console.log(set.has(4)); // false
```

A Map is a collection of key-value pairs, where each key is unique. You can create a Map by using the Mapconstructor.

Here's an example of how to create a Map and add items to it:

```
var map = new Map();
map.set("name", "John");
map.set("age", 30);
```

You can use the size property to get the number of items in a Map, and the get method to get the value of a specific key.

Here's an example of how to use the size property and the get method:

```
console.log(map.size); // 2
console.log(map.get("name")); // "John"
```

A WeakMap is similar to a Map, but it only holds weak references to its keys, meaning that the keys can be garbage collected if there are no other references to them. This makes WeakMaps useful for storing data that you want to be automatically cleaned up when it is no longer needed.

To create a WeakMap, you need to use the WeakMap constructor and pass in an iterable of key-value pairs.

Here's an example of how to create a WeakMap and add items to it:

```
var weakMap = new WeakMap([
  [{}, "value1"],
  [{}, "value2"]
]);
```

You can use the get method to retrieve the value of a specific key in a WeakMap.

Here's an example of how to use the get method to retrieve a value from a WeakMap:

```
var value = weakMap.get(key); // "value"
```

Note that WeakMaps do not have a size property or a has method, so you cannot get the number of items in a WeakMap or check if a WeakMap contains a specific key.

Conclusion

In this article, we've covered the different types of arrays and collections in JavaScript and how to use them to store and manipulate data. By understanding how to work with arrays and collections, you'll have the skills you need to create efficient and effective data structures for your JavaScript applications.

Exercises

To review these concepts, we will go through a series of exercises designed to test your understanding and apply what you have learned.

Create an array of numbers and use a loop to print the square of each number to the console.

Create a Set of strings and use the forEach method to print each string to the console.

Create an array of objects and use the forEach method to print the name of each object to the console.

Create a Set of numbers and use the size property and the has method to check if the set contains the number 5.

Create a Map of key-value pairs and use the get method to retrieve the value of the key "key1".

Solutions

Create an array of numbers and use a loop to print the square of each number to the console.

```
var numbers = [1, 2, 3, 4, 5];
numbers.forEach(function(number) {
  console.log(number * number);
});
```

Create a Set of strings and use the forEach method to print each string to the console.

```
var set = new Set(["apple", "banana", "cherry"]);
set.forEach(function(item) {
  console.log(item);
});
```

Create an array of objects and use the forEach method to print the name of each object to the console.

```
var objects = [
  {name: "John"},
  {name: "Jane"},
  {name: "Jim"}
];
objects.forEach(function(object) {
  console.log(object.name);
});
```

Create a Set of numbers and use the size property and the has method to check if the set contains the number 5.

```
var set = new Set([1, 2, 3, 4, 5]);
console.log(set.size); // 5
console.log(set.has(5)); // true
```

Create a Map of key-value pairs and use the get method to retrieve the value of the key "key1".

```
var map = new Map([
```

```
  ["key1", "value1"],
  ["key2", "value2"]
]);
console.log(map.get("key1")); // "value1"
```

ASYNCHRONOUS PROGRAMMING WITH PROMISES AND ASYNC/AWAIT

Asynchronous programming is an important concept in JavaScript, as it allows you to perform long-running tasks without blocking the main thread of execution. In this article, we'll go over the basics of asynchronous programming in JavaScript, and how to use promises and the async/await syntax to make it easier to work with asynchronous code.

What is Asynchronous Programming?

Asynchronous programming is a programming paradigm in which a program can perform multiple tasks concurrently, rather than sequentially. This allows a program to perform multiple tasks simultaneously, without having to wait for one task to complete before starting another.

In JavaScript, asynchronous programming is often used when working with I/O operations, such as reading or writing to a file, or making an HTTP request to a server. These types of operations can take a long time to complete, and blocking the main thread of execution while they are running can lead to a poor user experience. By using asynchronous programming, you can perform these tasks concurrently, without blocking the main thread of execution.

Callbacks

One of the earliest approaches to asynchronous programming in JavaScript was to use callback functions. A callback function is a function that is passed as an argument to another function, and is called when the task that the function performs has completed.

Here's an example of how to use a callback function to make an HTTP request:

```javascript
function makeRequest(url, callback) {
  // Make the request
  var xhr = new XMLHttpRequest();
  xhr.open("GET", url);
  xhr.onload = function() {
    callback(xhr.responseText);
  };
  xhr.send();
```

```
}
// Use the callback function
makeRequest("http://example.com", function(response) {
  console.log(response);
});
```

While callback functions are effective at handling asynchronous tasks, they can lead to what is known as "callback hell" if you have multiple asynchronous tasks that depend on each other. This can result in a deep nesting of callback functions, which can be difficult to read and maintain.

Promises

To address the issue of "callback hell," JavaScript introduced promises in ECMAScript 2015 (ES6). A promise is an object that represents the result of an asynchronous operation. A promise can be in one of three states:

- **Pending**: The promise has not yet been fulfilled or rejected.
- **Fulfilled**: The promise has been fulfilled, and the asynchronous operation was successful.
- **Rejected**: The promise has been rejected, and the asynchronous operation failed.

Promises provide a more declarative and readable way to handle asynchronous operations. Instead of using callback functions, you can use the then and catch methods of a promise to specify what should happen when the promise is fulfilled or rejected.

Here's an example of how to use a promise to make an HTTP request:

```
function makeRequest(url) {
  return new Promise(function(resolve, reject) {
    // Make the request
    var xhr = new XMLHttpRequest();
    xhr.open("GET", url);
    xhr.onload = function() {
      if (xhr.status === 200) {
        resolve(xhr.responseText);
      } else {
        reject(xhr.statusText);
      }
    };
    xhr.send();
  });
}
// Use the then and catch methods
```

```
makeRequest("http://example.com")
.then(function(response) {
  console.log(response);
})
.catch(function(error) {
  console.error(error);
});
```

async/await

The async/await syntax is a newer addition to JavaScript that makes it even easier to work with asynchronous code. The async keyword is used to declare an asynchronous function, and the awaitkeyword is used to wait for a promise to be fulfilled or rejected before continuing execution.

Here's an example of how to use the async/await syntax to make an HTTP request:

```
async function makeRequest(url) {
// Make the request
var xhr = new XMLHttpRequest();
xhr.open("GET", url);
xhr.onload = function() {
  if (xhr.status === 200) {
    return xhr.responseText;
  } else {
    throw new Error(xhr.statusText);
  }
};
xhr.send();
}
// Use the await keyword
try {
var response = await makeRequest("http://example.com");
console.log(response);
} catch (error) {
console.error(error);
}
```

Using the async/await syntax makes asynchronous code feel more like synchronous code, which can make it easier to read and understand.

Conclusion

In this article, we've covered the basics of asynchronous programming in JavaScript, and how to use promises and the async/await syntax to make it easier to work with asynchronous code. By understanding how to work with asynchronous programming, you'll have the skills you need to create efficient and effective JavaScript applications that can handle long-running tasks without blocking the main thread of execution.

Exercises

To review these concepts, we will go through a series of exercises designed to test your understanding and apply what you have learned.

Use a promise to make an HTTP request to retrieve a JSON file, and parse the JSON data using JSON.parse.

Use the async/await **syntax to make an HTTP request to retrieve a JSON file, and parse the JSON data using** JSON.parse.

Use a promise to make an HTTP request to retrieve a file, and use the FileReader **API to read the file as text.**

Use the async/await **syntax to make an HTTP request to retrieve a file, and use the** FileReader **API to read the file as text.**

Use a promise to make an HTTP request to retrieve a JSON file, parse the JSON data using JSON.parse, **and use the** map **method to transform the data into an array of objects with a** name **property.**

Solutions

Use a promise to make an HTTP request to retrieve a JSON file, and parse the JSON data using JSON.parse.

```javascript
function getJSON(url) {
  return new Promise(function(resolve, reject) {
    // Make the request
    var xhr = new XMLHttpRequest();
    xhr.open("GET", url);
    xhr.onload = function() {
      if (xhr.status === 200) {
        resolve(JSON.parse(xhr.responseText));
      } else {
        reject(xhr.statusText);
      }
    };
    xhr.send();
  });
}
```

```
getJSON("http://example.com/data.json")
.then(function(data) {
  console.log(data);
})
.catch(function(error) {
  console.error(error);
});
```

Use the async/await **syntax to make an HTTP request to retrieve a JSON file, and parse the JSON data using** JSON.parse.

```
async function getJSON(url) {
// Make the request
var xhr = new XMLHttpRequest();
xhr.open("GET", url);
xhr.onload = function() {
  if (xhr.status === 200) {
    return JSON.parse(xhr.responseText);
  } else {
    throw new Error(xhr.statusText);
  }
};
xhr.send();
}
try {
var data = await getJSON("http://example.com/data.json");
  console.log(data);
} catch (error) {
  console.error(error);
}
```

Use a promise to make an HTTP request to retrieve a file, and use the FileReader **API to read the file as text.**

```
function getFile(url) {
  return new Promise(function(resolve, reject) {
  // Make the request
  var xhr = new XMLHttpRequest();
  xhr.open("GET", url);
```

```
xhr.responseType = "blob";
xhr.onload = function() {
  if (xhr.status === 200) {
    resolve(xhr.response);
  } else {
    reject(xhr.statusText);
  }
};
xhr.send();
});
}
getFile("http://example.com/file.txt")
.then(function(file) {
  var reader = new FileReader();
  reader.onload = function() {
    console.log(reader.result);
  };
  reader.readAsText(file);
})
.catch(function(error) {
  console.error(error);
});
```

Use the async/await **syntax to make an HTTP request to retrieve a file, and use the** FileReader **API to read the file as text.**

```
async function getFile(url) {
  // Make the request
  var xhr = new XMLHttpRequest();
  xhr.open("GET", url);
  xhr.responseType = "blob";
  xhr.onload = function() {
    if (xhr.status === 200) {
      return xhr.response;
    } else {
      throw new Error(xhr.statusText);
    }
  };
```

```
 xhr.send();
}
try {
 var file = await getFile("http://example.com/file.txt");
 var reader = new FileReader();
 reader.onload = function() {
  console.log(reader.result);
 };
 reader.readAsText(file);
} catch (error) {
 console.error(error);
}
```

Use a promise to make an HTTP request to retrieve a JSON file, parse the JSON data using JSON.parse, and use the map method to transform the data into an array of objects with a name property.

```
function getJSON(url) {
 return new Promise(function(resolve, reject) {
  // Make the request
  var xhr = new XMLHttpRequest();
  xhr.open("GET", url);
  xhr.onload = function() {
   if (xhr.status === 200) {
    resolve(JSON.parse(xhr.responseText));
   } else {
    reject(xhr.statusText);
   }
  };
  xhr.send();
 });
}
getJSON("http://example.com/data.json")
.then(function(data) {
  return data.map(function(item) {
   return {name: item.name};
  });
})
```

```
.then(function(data) {
  console.log(data);
})
.catch(function(error) {
  console.error(error);
});
```

WORKING WITH APIS AND AJAX REQUESTS

In this chapter of the "Learn JavaScript" course, we will be exploring how to work with APIs (Application Programming Interfaces) and make AJAX (Asynchronous JavaScript and XML) requests in JavaScript. APIs allow you to access data and functionality from other websites and services, and AJAX allows you to make requests to APIs asynchronously, without the need to refresh the page.

What is an API?

An API is a set of rules that defines how two systems can communicate with each other. APIs allow you to access data and functionality from other websites and services, and can be accessed using HTTP requests.

There are many APIs available on the web, and they can be used to access a wide range of data and functionality. Some examples of what you can do with APIs include:

- Retrieve data from a database or service
- Add or update data in a database or service
- Perform a specific action (e.g. sending an email or posting to social media)

APIs often require you to authenticate your request using an API key or other form of authentication. It is also common for APIs to have rate limits, which limit the number of requests you can make within a certain time period.

Making API requests with JavaScript

To make API requests in JavaScript, you can use the XMLHttpRequest object or the fetch function.

The XMLHttpRequest object is a legacy API that has been around since the early days of the web. It allows you to make HTTP requests and receive responses asynchronously, without the need to refresh the page. Here's an example of how to use the XMLHttpRequest object to make a GET request to an API:

```javascript
function makeRequest(url) {
  var xhr = new XMLHttpRequest();
  xhr.open("GET", url);
  xhr.onload = function() {
    if (xhr.status === 200) {
      console.log(xhr.responseText);
```

```
  } else {
    console.error(xhr.statusText);
  }
};
xhr.send();
}
makeRequest("http://example.com/api/data");
```

The fetch function is a newer API that was introduced in JavaScript with the fetch API. It allows you to make HTTP requests and receive responses asynchronously, and returns a promise that resolves to a Response object. Here's an example of how to use the fetch function to make a GET request to an API:

```
fetch("http://example.com/api/data")
.then(function(response) {
  return response.text();
})
.then(function(data) {
  console.log(data);
})
.catch(function(error) {
  console.error(error);
});
```

Both the XMLHttpRequest object and the fetch function allow you to make other types of HTTP requests, such as POST, PUT, DELETE, etc., by setting the method property of the request.

Working with JSON data

Many APIs return data in JSON (JavaScript Object Notation) format, which is a lightweight data interchange format that is easy for humans to read and write, and easy for machines to parse and generate.

To parse JSON data in JavaScript, you can use the JSON.parse function. Here's an example of how to parse JSON data using the JSON.parse function:

```
var jsonData = '{"name": "John", "age": 30, "city": "New York"}';
var data = JSON.parse(jsonData);
console.log(data.name); // "John"
console.log(data.age); // 30
console.log(data.city); // "New York"
```

To convert a JavaScript object or array into a JSON string, you can use the JSON.stringify function. Here's an example of how to convert a JavaScript object into a JSON string using the JSON.stringifyfunction:

```
var data = {name: "John", age: 30, city: "New York"};
var jsonData = JSON.stringify(data);
console.log(jsonData); // '{"name":"John","age":30,"city":"New York"}'
```

Working with AJAX requests

AJAX (Asynchronous JavaScript and XML) is a term used to describe the process of making asynchronous HTTP requests and receiving responses in JavaScript, without the need to refresh the page. AJAX allows you to update parts of a webpage dynamically, by making requests to an API and updating the DOM (Document Object Model) with the response.

To make an AJAX request in JavaScript, you can use the XMLHttpRequest object or the fetch function, as we discussed earlier. Here's an example of how to make an AJAX request using the XMLHttpRequest object:

```
function makeRequest(url) {
  var xhr = new XMLHttpRequest();
  xhr.open("GET", url);
  xhr.onload = function() {
    if (xhr.status === 200) {
      var data = JSON.parse(xhr.responseText);
      // Update the DOM with the response data
    } else {
      console.error(xhr.statusText);
    }
  };
  xhr.send();
}

// Make the AJAX request when the button is clicked
var button = document.getElementById("button");
button.addEventListener("click", function() {
  makeRequest("http://example.com/api/data");
});
```

Here's an example of how to make an AJAX request using the fetch function:

```
function makeRequest(url) {
  fetch(url)
    .then(function(response) {
      return response.json();
```

```
})
.then(function(data) {
  // Update the DOM with the response data
})
.catch(function(error) {
  console.error(error);
});
}
// Make the AJAX request when the button is clicked
var button = document.getElementById("button");
button.addEventListener("click", function() {
  makeRequest("http://example.com/api/data");
});
```

Conclusion

In this chapter of the "Learn JavaScript" course, we learned about APIs and how to make AJAX requests in JavaScript. We also learned how to work with JSON data, and how to use the XMLHttpRequest object and the fetch function to make HTTP requests and receive responses asynchronously.

By understanding how to work with APIs and make AJAX requests, you can build dynamic, interactive web applications that can access and manipulate data from other websites and services.

Exercises

To review these concepts, we will go through a series of exercises designed to test your understanding and apply what you have learned.

Make an AJAX request to the **GitHub API** to retrieve the list of repositories for a given user, and display the repository names in a list on the page.

Make an AJAX request to the **OpenWeatherMap API** to retrieve the current weather for a given city, and display the temperature and weather description on the page.

Make an AJAX request to the **Wikipedia API** to search for articles with a given keyword, and display the article titles and descriptions in a list on the page.

Make an AJAX request to the **NASA Astronomy Picture of the Day API** to retrieve the current "Astronomy Picture of the Day," and display the image and description on the page.

Make an AJAX request to the **USGS Earthquake API** to retrieve a list of earthquakes in the past week, and display the earthquake magnitudes and locations on a map using the **Google Maps API**.

Solutions

Make an AJAX request to the GitHub API to retrieve the list of repositories for a given user, and display the repository names in a list on the page.

```
function getRepos(username) {
fetch(`https://api.github.com/users/${username}/repos`)
.then(function(response) {
return response.json();
})
.then(function(repos) {
var list = document.getElementById("repo-list");
repos.forEach(function(repo) {
var li = document.createElement("li");
li.textContent = repo.name;
list.appendChild(li);
});
})
.catch(function(error) {
console.error(error);
});
}
var button = document.getElementById("button");
button.addEventListener("click", function() {
var username = document.getElementById("username").value;
getRepos(username);
});
```

Make an AJAX request to the **OpenWeatherMap API** to retrieve the current weather for a given city, and display the temperature and weather description on the page.

```
function getWeather(city) {
fetch(`https://api.openweathermap.org/data/2.5/weather?q=${city}&appid=YOUR_API_KEY`)
.then(function(response) {
return response.json();
})
.then(function(data) {
var temperature = data.main.temp;
var description = data.weather[0].description;
document.getElementById("temperature").textContent = temperature;
document.getElementById("description").textContent = description;
})
.catch(function(error) {
```

```javascript
    console.error(error);
  });
}
var button = document.getElementById("button");
button.addEventListener("click", function() {
 var city = document.getElementById("city").value;
 getWeather(city);
});
```

Make an AJAX request to the **Wikipedia API** to search for articles with a given keyword, and display the article titles and descriptions in a list on the page.

```javascript
function searchArticles(keyword) {
                              fetch(`https://en.wikipedia.org/w/api.php?action=query&format=json&list=search&utf8=1&formatversion=2&srsearch=${keyword}`)
  .then(function(response) {
   return response.json();
  })
  .then(function(data) {
   var list = document.getElementById("article-list");
   data.query.search.forEach(function(article) {
    var li = document.createElement("li");
    var a = document.createElement("a");
    a.textContent = article.title;
    a.href = `https://en.wikipedia.org/wiki/${article.title}`;
    li.appendChild(a);
    li.appendChild(document.createTextNode(` - ${article.snippet}`));
    list.appendChild(li);
   });
  })
  .catch(function(error) {
   console.error(error);
  });
}
var button = document.getElementById("button");
button.addEventListener("click", function() {
 var keyword = document.getElementById("keyword").value;
 searchArticles(keyword);
```

```
});
```

Make an AJAX request to the **NASA Astronomy Picture of the Day API to retrieve the current "Astronomy Picture of the Day," and display the image and description on the page.**

```
function getAPOD() {
  var apiKey = "YOUR_API_KEY";
  fetch(`https://api.nasa.gov/planetary/apod?api_key=${apiKey}`)
    .then(function(response) {
      return response.json();
    })
    .then(function(data) {
      var img = document.getElementById("apod-img");
      img.src = data.url;
      img.alt = data.title;
      document.getElementById("apod-title").textContent = data.title;
      document.getElementById("apod-description").textContent = data.explanation;
    })
    .catch(function(error) {
      console.error(error);
    });
}
getAPOD();
```

Make an AJAX request to the **USGS Earthquake API to retrieve a list of earthquakes in the past week, and display the earthquake magnitudes and locations on a map using the Google Maps API.** First, you'll need to obtain an API key for the Google Maps API by following the instructions on the Google Maps API documentation. Then, you can use the following code to make the AJAX request to the USGS Earthquake API and display the earthquakes on a map:

```
function initMap() {
  var map = new google.maps.Map(document.getElementById("map"), {
    zoom: 2,
    center: {lat: 0, lng: 0}
  });
  fetch("https://earthquake.usgs.gov/fdsnws/event/1/query?format=geojson&starttime=2022-01-01&endtime=2022-01-08")
    .then(function(response) {
      return response.json();
    })
```

```
.then(function(data) {
data.features.forEach(function(earthquake) {
var marker = new google.maps.Marker({
position: earthquake.geometry.coordinates,
map: map,
title: `Magnitude ${earthquake.properties.mag} - ${earthquake.properties.place}`
});
});
})
.catch(function(error) {
console.error(error);
});
}
```

PUTTING EVERYTHING TOGETHER TO BUILD A WEB APP USING JAVASCRIPT

Now that you've learned the fundamentals of JavaScript, it's time to put everything together and build a web app. In this final chapter of the "Learn JavaScript" course, you'll learn how to use JavaScript to build interactive, dynamic web applications that can communicate with servers, access data, and perform complex tasks.

Setting up a Development Environment

Before you start building your web app, you'll need to set up a development environment. This includes installing a code editor, setting up a local development server, and configuring your project structure.

There are many code editors to choose from, such as **Sublime Text**, **Atom**, and **Visual Studio Code**. These code editors provide features such as syntax highlighting, code completion, and debugging tools to make it easier to write and debug your code.

To set up a local development server, you can use tools such as **XAMPP**, **WAMP**, or **MAMP**. These tools allow you to run a web server on your local machine, which is useful for testing and debugging your web app before deploying it to a live server.

Once you have a code editor and development server set up, you'll need to decide on a project structure for your web app. A common structure is to have a css directory for your stylesheets, a js directory for your JavaScript files, and an index.html file for your HTML. You may also want to include directories for images, fonts, and other assets.

Building the HTML Structure

The first step in building a web app is to create the HTML structure. This includes defining the layout of your app, adding elements such as headers, footers, and navigation, and marking up the content with HTML tags.

To create the layout of your app, you can use HTML5 structural tags such as header, footer, and main. You can also use CSS to style your app and define the layout using layout properties such as display, flexbox, and grid.

To add navigation to your app, you can use an unordered list with li elements and a nav element. You can also use a button element or a select element to create a dropdown menu.

To mark up your content, you can use a variety of HTML tags such as h1, p, a, and img. You can also use semantic HTML tags such as article, section, and aside to give meaning to your content and make it more accessible to screen readers and search engines.

Adding Interactivity with JavaScript

Once you have the HTML structure of your web app in place, you can start adding interactivity with JavaScript. This includes responding to user events such as clicks, hover, and form submissions, manipulating the DOM to change the content and layout of your app, and making AJAX requests to access data from external sources.

To respond to user events, you can use event listeners such as click, hover, and submit. You can also use the addEventListener method to attach event listeners to elements in your HTML.

To manipulate the DOM, you can use JavaScript methods such as getElementById, querySelector, and createElement to access and modify elements in your HTML. You can use properties such as innerHTML, style, and classList to change the content and appearance of elements, and you can use methods such as appendChild and removeChild to add and remove elements from the DOM.

To make AJAX requests, you can use the fetch function or the XMLHttpRequest object to send HTTP requests to external servers. You can use these requests to access data from APIs, load content from other pages, or submit form data to the server.

Putting it all Together

To build a complete web app, you'll need to combine all of these elements and use them to create a cohesive, interactive user experience. This may involve using HTML and CSS to design a user interface, using JavaScript to add interactivity and functionality, and using AJAX to access data and communicate with servers.

To test and debug your web app, you can use the development tools in your code editor and browser to inspect the HTML, CSS, and JavaScript, and to identify and fix errors. You can also use console.log statements to output debug messages and test your code.

Conclusion

Building a web app requires a combination of HTML, CSS, and JavaScript skills. By following the steps outlined in this chapter, you should have a solid foundation for building your own web app using JavaScript. Whether you're creating a simple to-do list app or a complex web application, the concepts and techniques covered in this course will serve as a useful starting point.

Example Project

For this sample project, we'll build a simple to-do list app using HTML, CSS, and JavaScript. The app will allow users to add, remove, and mark tasks as complete.

To get started, we'll set up the HTML structure of the app. We'll create a div element with an id of "todo-list" to contain the list of tasks, and we'll create a form element with an id of "add-task-form" to allow users to add new tasks. Inside the form, we'll add a input element with a type of "text" to allow users to enter the task title, and a button element with a type of "submit" to submit the form.

```html
<div id="todo-list">
 <ul>
 </ul>
</div>
<form id="add-task-form">
 <input type="text" id="task-title" placeholder="Enter task title">
 <button type="submit">Add Task</button>
</form>
```

Next, we'll write the CSS to style the app. We'll use a combination of layout properties such as displayand flexbox to define the layout of the app, and we'll use color and font properties to style the elements.

```css
#todo-list {
 display: flex;
 flex-direction: column;
 width: 400px;
 margin: 0 auto;
}
#add-task-form {
 display: flex;
 align-items: center;
 margin-bottom: 20px;
}
#add-task-form input[type="text"] {
 flex-grow: 1;
 padding: 8px;
 font-size: 16px;
 border: none;
 border-radius: 4px;
}
#add-task-form button[type="submit"] {
 margin-left: 10px;
 padding: 8px;
 font-size: 16px;
```

```css
  background-color: #00b8d4;
  color: white;
  border: none;
  border-radius: 4px;
  cursor: pointer;
}
#todo-list ul {
  list-style: none;
  margin: 0;
  padding: 0;
}
#todo-list li {
  display: flex;
  align-items: center;
  padding: 8px;
  border-radius: 4px;
  margin-bottom: 8px;
  background-color: #f1f1f1;
}
#todo-list li.completed {
  background-color: #ccc;
  text-decoration: line-through;
}
#todo-list li .task-title {
  flex-grow: 1;
  font-size: 16px;
}
#todo-list li .delete-button {
  margin-left: 10px;
  font-size: 16px;
  color: #ff6b6b;
  cursor: pointer;
}
```

Finally, we'll write the JavaScript to add the interactivity to the app. We'll use the `addEventListener` method to attach event listeners to the form and the delete buttons, and we'll use DOM manipulation methods to add, remove, and modify elements in the HTML.

```javascript
// Get references to the form and list elements
const form = document.querySelector("#add-task-form");
const taskList = document.querySelector("#todo-list ul");
// Add a submit event listener to the form
form.addEventListener("submit", e => {
  // Prevent the form from submitting
  e.preventDefault();
  // Get the task title from the input element
  const taskTitle = document.querySelector("#task-title").value;
  // Create a new list item element
  const taskItem = document.createElement("li");
  // Add a class of "completed" if the task is completed
  taskItem.classList.add("completed");
  // Set the innerHTML of the task item to the task title
  taskItem.innerHTML = `
    <span class="task-title">${taskTitle}</span>
    <button class="delete-button">Delete</button>
  `;
  // Append the task item to the task list
  taskList.appendChild(taskItem);
  // Clear the task title input
  document.querySelector("#task-title").value = "";
});
// Add a click event listener to the task list
taskList.addEventListener("click", e => {
  // Get the target element that was clicked
  const target = e.target;
  // If the target is a delete button, delete the task
  if (target.classList.contains("delete-button")) {
    target.parentElement.remove();
  }
  // If the target is the task title, toggle the completed class
  if (target.classList.contains("task-title")) {
    target.parentElement.classList.toggle("completed");
  }
}
```

```
});
```

With these HTML, CSS, and JavaScript pieces in place, we now have a functioning to-do list app that allows users to add, remove, and mark tasks as complete.

WORKING WITH LIBRARIES AND FRAMEWORKS (JQUERY, REACT, ETC.)

As you continue to develop web applications with JavaScript, you may find that you need to use libraries and frameworks to help streamline your development process and add advanced features to your apps. In this chapter, we'll explore some of the most popular libraries and frameworks for JavaScript, including jQuery, React, and Angular.

What are Libraries and Frameworks?

A library is a collection of pre-written code that provides utility functions and other helpful tools for a specific purpose. A framework is a more comprehensive structure that provides a set of conventions and guidelines for building applications. Both libraries and frameworks can be used to save time and effort when developing applications, but they differ in the level of abstraction and the amount of control they provide.

jQuery

jQuery is a popular library that provides a set of utility functions and methods for interacting with the DOM, making HTTP requests, and animating elements. One of the main benefits of jQuery is that it simplifies common JavaScript tasks and allows you to write shorter, more concise code.

To use jQuery, you'll need to include the jQuery library in your HTML file. You can either download the library and include it locally, or you can include it from a CDN (Content Delivery Network) by adding a script tag to your HTML file.

```
<script
src="https://code.jquery.com/jquery-3.6.0.min.js">
</script>
```

Once the library is included, you can start using jQuery by selecting elements from the DOM and applying functions and methods to them. For example, to select all the p elements on a page and hide them, you can use the hidefunction:

```
$("p").hide();
```

jQuery also provides a set of events that you can use to respond to user actions such as clicks, hovers, and form submissions. For example, to attach a click event to a button, you can use the click function:

```
$("button").click(function() {
  // code to execute when the button is clicked
});
```

React

React is a JavaScript library for building user interfaces. It was developed by Facebook and is now maintained by a community of developers. React allows you to create reusable components that can be easily combined to build complex applications.

One of the main benefits of React is that it uses a virtual DOM (Document Object Model) to optimize updates to the actual DOM. This means that when the state of a component changes, React will only update the parts of the DOM that are necessary, rather than rebuilding the entire DOM tree. This can greatly improve the performance of your application, especially when working with large datasets or frequently changing data.

To use React, you'll need to include the React library in your HTML file and set up a build process to compile your code. There are several ways to do this, but one popular method is to use the create-react-app tool, which sets up a development environment with a configuration that includes Webpack, Babel, and other tools.

Once you have React set up, you can start creating components. A component is a piece of code that represents a part of a user interface. You can define a component using a JavaScript class or function, and you can use JSX (JavaScript XML) syntax to define the HTML-like structure of the component.

Here's an example of a component that displays a list of items:

```
import React from "react";
class List extends React.Component {
  render() {
    return (
      <ul>
        <li>Item 1</li>
        <li>Item 2</li>
        <li>Item 3</li>
      </ul>
    );
  }
}
```

To use the component, you can include it in your HTML file like this:

```
<div id="root"></div>
```

And you can render the component to the root element using the ReactDOM.render method:

```
import React from "react";
import ReactDOM from "react-dom";
import List from "./List";
ReactDOM.render(<List />, document.getElementById("root"));
```

React components can also have state and props (properties). State is a way to manage data that can change within a component, and props are a way to pass data from a parent component to a child component.

For example, here's a component that has a stateful value and a prop that controls the color of the text:

```
import React from "react";
class Counter extends React.Component {
 constructor(props) {
  super(props);
  this.state = {
   count: 0
  };
 }
 render() {
  return (
   <div>
    <p style={{ color: this.props.color }}>
     The count is {this.state.count}.
    </p>
    <button onClick={() => this.setState({ count: this.state.count + 1 })}>
     Increment
    </button>
   </div>
  );
 }
}
```

To use the component, you can pass a value for the color prop like this:

```
ReactDOM.render(
 <Counter color="#00b8d4" />,
 document.getElementById("root")
);
```

Angular

Angular is a full-featured framework for building single-page applications. It provides a set of conventions and tools for creating complex applications with a modular architecture.

Angular uses a component-based architecture, similar to React, but it also provides additional features such as dependency injection, routing, and a built-in HTTP client. It also has a templating syntax called HTML templates, which allows you to define the structure of your components using HTML-like syntax.

To use Angular, you'll need to include the Angular library in your HTML file and set up a build process to compile your code. You can use the Angular CLI (Command Line Interface) tool to set up a development environment and create a new Angular project.

Once you have Angular set up, you can start creating components. A component in Angular is a class that defines the properties and behavior of a view element. You can use the @Component decorator to define the component, and you can use the template or templateUrl property to define the HTML template for the component.

Here's an example of a simple component that displays a greeting:

```
import { Component } from "@angular/core";
@Component({
  selector: "app-greeting",
  template: `
    <h1>Hello, World!</h1>
  `
})
export class GreetingComponent {
  // component logic goes here
}
```

To use the component, you can include it in your HTML file like this:

```
<app-greeting></app-greeting>
```

Angular components can also have inputs and outputs, which allow you to pass data between components. For example, here's a component that has an input for a user name and an output that fires an event when the user clicks a button:

```
import { Component, Input, Output, EventEmitter } from "@angular/core";
@Component({
  selector: "app-user",
  template: `
    <p>{{ userName }}</p>
```

```
  <button (click)="onClick()">Click me</button>
  `
})
export class UserComponent {
  @Input() userName: string;
  @Output() clicked = new EventEmitter<void>();
  onClick() {
    this.clicked.emit();
  }
}
```

To use the component, you can bind to the userName input and listen to the clicked output like this:

```
<app-user [userName]="'John'" (clicked)="handleClick()"></app-user>
```

Angular also provides a powerful routing system that allows you to define multiple routes for your application and navigate between them. You can define routes using the RouterModule and the Routes array.

For example, here's how you can define two routes for an application:

```
import { NgModule } from "@angular/core";
import { RouterModule, Routes } from "@angular/router";
import { HomeComponent } from "./home.component";
import { AboutComponent } from "./about.component";
const routes: Routes = [
  { path: "", component: HomeComponent },
  { path: "about", component: AboutComponent }
];
@NgModule({
  imports: [RouterModule.forRoot(routes)],
  exports: [RouterModule]
})
export class AppRoutingModule {}
```

You can then use the routerLink directive to create links to the different routes, and you can use the router-outlet directive to define where the content for the current route will be displayed.

```
<nav>
  <a routerLink="/">Home</a>
  <a routerLink="/about">About</a>
</nav>
```

```
<router-outlet></router-outlet>
```

Conclusion

Libraries and frameworks can greatly improve your productivity when developing applications with JavaScript. They provide a set of tools and conventions that can help you write cleaner, more maintainable code and build more complex applications faster. In this chapter, we've explored some of the most popular libraries and frameworks, including jQuery, React, and Angular. Whether you choose to use a library or a framework will depend on your specific needs and preferences, but either way, you'll be able to take advantage of the powerful capabilities that these tools provide.

Exercises

To review these concepts, we will go through a series of exercises designed to test your understanding and apply what you have learned.

Write a jQuery function that selects all the p elements on a page and toggles their visibility when a button is clicked.

Write a React component that displays a form with two input fields (email and password) and a submit button. When the form is submitted, display an alert with the values of the input fields.

Write an Angular component that displays a list of users, each with a name and an avatar. The component should have an input for a list of users and an output that fires an event when a user is clicked.

Write a jQuery function that makes an AJAX request to a REST API and displays the result in a table.

Write a React component that uses the useEffect hook to fetch data from a REST API and display it in a list.

Solutions

Write a jQuery function that selects all the p elements on a page and toggles their visibility when a button is clicked.

```
$(document).ready(function() {
  $("button").click(function() {
    $("p").toggle();
  });
});
```

Write a React component that displays a form with two input fields (email and password) and a submit button. When the form is submitted, display an alert with the values of the input fields.

```
import React from "react";
class Form extends React.Component {
  handleSubmit(event) {
    event.preventDefault();
    const email = event.target.elements.email.value;
```

```
    const password = event.target.elements.password.value;

    alert(`Email: ${email} Password: ${password}`);

}

render() {

  return (

    <form onSubmit={this.handleSubmit}>

      <label>

        Email:

        <input type="email" name="email" />

      </label>

      <br />

      <label>

        Password:

        <input type="password" name="password" />

      </label>

      <br />

      <button type="submit">Submit</button>

    </form>

  );

}

}
```

Write an Angular component that displays a list of users, each with a name and an avatar. The component should have an input for a list of users and an output that fires an event when a user is clicked.

```
import { Component, Input, Output, EventEmitter } from "@angular/core";

@Component({

selector: "app-user-list",

template: `

  <ul>

    <li *ngFor="let user of users" (click)="handleClick(user)">

      {{ user.name }}

      <img [src]="user.avatarUrl" [alt]="user.name" />

    </li>

  </ul>

`

})
```

```
export class UserListComponent {
 @Input() users: any[];
 @Output() userClicked = new EventEmitter<any>();
 handleClick(user) {
   this.userClicked.emit(user);
 }
}
```

Write a jQuery function that makes an AJAX request to a REST API and displays the result in a table.

```
$(document).ready(function() {
 $.ajax({
  url: "https://api.example.com/users",
  success: function(result) {
   const table = $("<table></table>");
   result.forEach(function(user) {
    const row = $("<tr></tr>");
    row.append(`<td>${user.name}</td>`);
    row.append(`<td>${user.email}</td>`);
    table.append(row);
   });
   $("#result").append(table);
  }
 });
});
```

Write a React component that uses the useEffect **hook to fetch data from a REST API and display it in a list.**

```
import React, { useEffect, useState } from "react";
function UserList() {
 const [users, setUsers] = useState([]);
 useEffect(() => {
  fetch("https://api.example.com/users")
   .then(response => response.json())
   .then(result => setUsers(result));
 }, []);
 return (
```

```
<ul>
 {users.map(user => (
  <li key={user.id}>{user.name}</li>
 ))}
 </ul>
);
}
```

DEBUGGING AND TROUBLESHOOTING JAVASCRIPT CODE

In addition to debugging, there are several other techniques that you can use to troubleshoot your JavaScript code.

Testing Your Code

Testing your code is a crucial part of the development process. It helps you ensure that your code is correct and works as expected under different conditions. There are several types of tests that you can use to validate your code, including unit tests, integration tests, and acceptance tests.

Unit tests are small, isolated tests that validate a specific piece of code, such as a function or a module. They are typically fast to run and allow you to test individual components in isolation.

Integration tests are tests that validate the interaction between multiple components. They are typically slower to run than unit tests and may require more setup and configuration.

Acceptance tests are tests that validate the overall functionality of your code from the perspective of the user. They may involve simulating user input and verifying that the expected output is produced.

To create tests for your JavaScript code, you can use a testing framework such as Jest or Mocha. These frameworks provide tools and conventions for writing and running tests and generating test reports.

Debugging Asynchronous Code

Asynchronous code is code that executes concurrently with the rest of your program. JavaScript uses an event-driven, single-threaded model to handle asynchronous code, which means that asynchronous code is executed in a separate execution context and can be triggered by events such as user input, timers, or network requests.

Debugging asynchronous code can be challenging because the order in which the code is executed may not be obvious. To debug asynchronous code, you can use the browser's developer console to view the call stack and set breakpoints. You can also use the console.log function to output intermediate values and trace the execution of your code.

Handling Errors

Errors are inevitable in software development, and it's important to handle them gracefully in your code. JavaScript provides several mechanisms for handling errors, including the try and catch statements and the throw statement.

The try and catch statements allow you to catch and handle exceptions that are thrown by your code. The try block contains the code that may throw an exception, and the catch block contains the code that will be executed if an exception is thrown.

```
try {
  // code that may throw an exception
} catch (error) {
  // code to handle the exception
}
```

The `throw` statement allows you to throw an exception manually. This can be useful for signaling an error condition or for controlling the flow of your code.

```
if (x > 100) {
  throw new Error("x is too big!");
}
```

When handling errors, it's important to choose the appropriate level of granularity. You should try to catch specific errors that you can handle and let other errors propagate up the call stack. You should also consider whether the error is recoverable or whether the program should terminate.

Debugging Third-Party Code

Sometimes you may encounter errors in third-party code, such as a library or a framework. Debugging third-party code can be challenging because you may not have access to the source code or documentation.

To debug third-party code, you can try the following techniques:

- Use the browser's developer console to inspect the state of your variables and the call stack.
- Use the console.log function to output intermediate values and trace the execution of the code.
- Use breakpoints to pause the execution of the code and inspect the state.
- Search online for documentation or solutions to common issues.
- Reach out to the maintainers of the code and ask for help.

Conclusion

Debugging and troubleshooting are important skills in software development. By using the tools and techniques discussed in this chapter, you can identify and fix issues in your JavaScript code and improve the quality and reliability of your code.

Exercises

To review these concepts, we will go through a series of exercises designed to test your understanding and apply what you have learned.

Write a function sum **that takes in two numbers as arguments and returns their sum. Use the** console.log **function to output the intermediate values of the variables and the final result.**

Write a function divide **that takes in two numbers as arguments and returns their quotient. Use the** try **and** catch **statements to handle the case where the second argument is 0. Use the** console.error **function to output the error message.**

Write a function parseInt **that takes in a string and returns the integer value of the string. Use the** console.log **function to output the intermediate values of the variables and the final result.**

Write a function sortArray **that takes in an array of numbers and returns a new array with the numbers sorted in ascending order. Use the** console.log **function to output the intermediate values of the variables and the final result.**

Write a function fetchData **that takes in a URL and returns a promise that resolves with the data from the URL. Use the** console.log **function to output the intermediate values of the variables and the final result.**

Solutions

Write a function sum **that takes in two numbers as arguments and returns their sum. Use the** console.log **function to output the intermediate values of the variables and the final result.**

```javascript
function sum(a, b) {
  console.log(`a: ${a}, b: ${b}`);
  const result = a + b;
  console.log(`result: ${result}`);
  return result;
}
console.log(sum(1, 2)); // output: 3
console.log(sum(5, 7)); // output: 12
```

Write a function divide **that takes in two numbers as arguments and returns their quotient. Use the** try **and** catch **statements to handle the case where the second argument is 0. Use the** console.error **function to output the error message.**

```javascript
function divide(a, b) {
  try {
    if (b === 0) {
      throw new Error("Cannot divide by 0");
    }
    return a / b;
  } catch (error) {
```

```
  console.error(error);
 }
}
console.log(divide(4, 2)); // output: 2
console.log(divide(4, 0)); // output: "Cannot divide by 0"
```

Write a function parseInt that takes in a string and returns the integer value of the string. Use the console.log function to output the intermediate values of the variables and the final result.

```
function parseInt(str) {
 console.log(`str: ${str}`);
 const result = Number.parseInt(str, 10);
 console.log(`result: ${result}`);
 return result;
}
console.log(parseInt("123")); // output: 123
console.log(parseInt("hello")); // output: NaN
```

Write a function sortArray that takes in an array of numbers and returns a new array with the numbers sorted in ascending order. Use the console.log function to output the intermediate values of the variables and the final result.

```
function sortArray(arr) {
 console.log(`arr: ${arr}`);
 const result = arr.sort((a, b) => a - b);
 console.log(`result: ${result}`);
 return result;
}
console.log(sortArray([5, 3, 1, 4, 2])); // output: [1, 2, 3, 4, 5]
console.log(sortArray([100, 50, 0, 25, 75])); // output: [0, 25, 50, 75, 100]
```

Write a function fetchData that takes in a URL and returns a promise that resolves with the data from the URL. Use the console.log function to output the intermediate values of the variables and the final result.

```
function fetchData(url) {
 console.log(`url: ${url}`);
 return fetch(url)
  .then(response => response.json())
```

THANK YOU

Thank you again for choosing "Learn JavaScript". I hope it helps you in your journey to learn JavaScript and achieve your goals. Please take a small portion of your time and share this with your friends and family and write a review for this book. I hope your programming journey does not end here. If you are interested, check out other books that I have or find more coding challenges at: https://codeofcode.org